pumpkins by ken robbins

Copyright © 2006 by Ken Robbins

A Neal Porter Book
Published by Roaring Brook Press
Roaring Brook Press is a division of
    Holtzbrinck Publishing Holdings Limited Partnership
175 Fifth Avenue, New York, New York 10010

Distributed in Canada by H. B. Fenn and Company, Ltd.

Library of Congress Cataloging-in-Publication Data
Robbins, Ken.
Pumpkins / by Ken Robbins.
p. cm.
"A Neal Porter book."
ISBN-13: 978-1-59643-184-3
ISBN-10: 1-59643-184-9
1. Pumpkin--Juvenile literature. I. Title.
SB347R62 2006
635'.62--dc22
2005033023

Roaring Brook Press books are available for special promotions and premiums.
For details, contact: Director of Special Markets, Holtzbrinck Publishers.

Printed in China

First edition August 2006

10 9 8 7

The author wishes to thank Lynne and Hank Kraszewski of Hank's Pumpkin Town, in
Watermill, N.Y.; Lynn Bistrian; the Halsey Family; Lisa and Bill Babinski of Lisa and Bill's
Fresh Vegetables, in Wainscott, N.Y.; Scott Armstrong, proud grower of a prize winning 1,064
pound pumpkin; The Bayberry Nursery of Amagansett, N.Y.; John Musnicki, pumpkin carver
extraordinaire, and most of all, Mr. Neal Porter, a real mensch.

pumpkins by ken robbins

A Neal Porter Book
ROARING BROOK PRESS
New York

At that time of year when the air has turned cool, the cornstalks have turned brown, and the leaves are falling, splashing their color on the ground . . .

and the geese are flying, and the crows are calling from the empty fields,
it seems there are pumpkins everywhere.

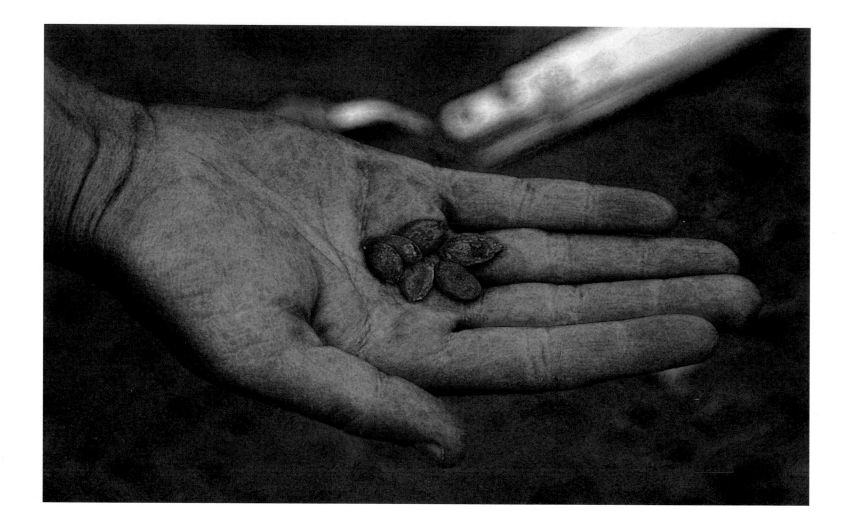

But the story of the pumpkin begins in the spring, when the farmer plants her seeds in the ground.

The first small leaves come up in ten days or so, and in just a few weeks the vines spread out and flower buds begin to show.

The buds open up and flowers appear.

At the base of a flower the pumpkin begins to grow.
It's green at first, but it soon changes color.

At the height of summer, full sized pumpkins are hidden among the vines. As the summer passes, the vines are cleared away, and a patchwork of pumpkins can be seen on the ground.

Pumpkins grow in any number of colors, and shapes, and sizes. The ones we know best are bright orange, and more or less round. But many kinds are yellow, tan, green, or even blue. Some are round, but some of them are kind of flattened, or squashed, you might say.

Some are so small they fit in your hand. Others are positively huge.

People hold contests to see who can grow the biggest ones.
The gigantic pumpkin on the forklift weighs over a thousand pounds.

Many farms will let you go out in their fields to pick your own pumpkin, right off the vine.

You must pay for it first, of course, and then you take it home.

For Halloween it's traditional to carve your pumpkin into a jack-o'-lantern.

You'll need a pen or marker that erases easily.
Draw a face—happy or scary—whatever you like.
Then get an ADULT to cut all around the top with a saw or knife.

Remove the top, and with your hands or a scoop, you can scrape out the
"guts" inside–the seeds and the wet membrane that holds them.
Then get that adult to cut out the eyes, the nose, and the mouth.

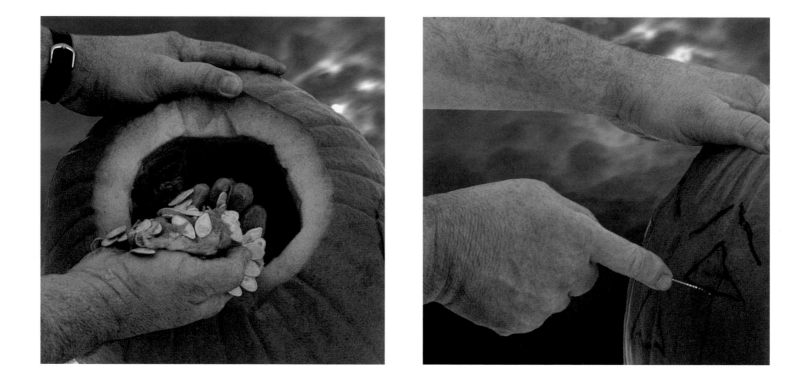

Once the jack-o'-lantern is carved, put it out on your steps at night, or in your
window, or in some other safe place. Put a candle inside and light it.
It will look quite nice.

On Halloween everyone dresses up for trick or treat.

Ghosts and goblins walk the streets, and pumpkins are a part of the scene.

By November, the pumpkins are mostly gone . . . picked for jack-o'-lanterns or pumpkin pie. The few that are left will die on the vine–eaten by animals or left to rot. Their seeds will survive–at least some of them will–to make more pumpkins the following year.